A PEACEFUL MIND
FOR ENTREPRENEURS

PRINCETON DRAKE

Dedication

This book is dedicated to the 15 year old kid who had a dream and some potential energy, that evolved to kinetic energy and has been in motion ever since. I feel it is my responsibility to pass along some great information that I garnered over this short span through my many experiences. May this short read uplift and propel the reader to a peaceful mind and elevated business. You deserve it all, put the work in. You deserve to be at peace, embrace the self. Mind, Body, Soul, coherence, alignment.

Rules For A Peaceful Mind As An Entrepreneur

1. Don't *EXPECT* customers to be loyal; *APPRECIATE* the loyal customers.

Throughout this build you may hear me bring this point back up a few times. Energy is something that can some times be hard to quantify and hard to define. I like to think of money as a way of quantifying and a result of energy that has been expelled. We work or exchange energy of some sort for the money or currency we have accumulated. Some people have done things they regret behind chasing money. Others go through the lowest points in their lives daily by simply going to a job to earn the money. Have we realized that we have been convinced to "pay" money to live on a free Earth? How many other species that inhabit this beautiful land have to pay to enjoy it? Some of us were raised to believe that the only way we can enjoy this life is after death. I mention all this to say that we can not EXPECT someone to spend their hard earned money with us and only us. We work too hard and endure too much on a daily basis to feel pressured or expected to spend with a specific person or group.

When we quantify the energy that we used over the week, there is typically some sort of contract or agreement that was made and we exchange energy for currency. When we have customers who choose to shop with you daily its because you have provided a product that suites them well. We typically build great client/customer relationships with these people as well. One of the highlights of my day is actually being able to interact with my customers. Relationships with people are your biggest source of currency, people are your largest source of currency! The exchange for energy can be represented by in my case, a plate of food for money we also converse about life and many other topics.

A personal connection and feeling to the individual is what builds the relationship that will result in a loyal customer. I once felt the emotion of anger and disappointment when the people closest to me would not support my business. It didn't take me long to come up with the phrase, "Expect Nothing, Appreciate Everything". This single phrase allowed me to release the expectation I had for individuals. I allow people to be. I allow them in my mind, from my perception to do and spend whatever it is with whomever they like. When we have an exception for others or things we tend to build a sense of disappointment that leads to resentment. Too many times have family members or friends create tension or friction because they expected me to spend my money with them and only them. Even when they were unqualified to do the job, they still expected me to bring the job to them. The fact is, I can do whatever it is I want in this world; I'm not hurting or affecting someone else negatively.

Another saying that has took the world by storm is "Treat others how you wish to be treated", to me this saying has caused people to expect the same in return when they do business and interact with others. In fact we should treat others how they want to be treated, not how we want to be treated. This dynamic shifts to a point where we expect others to respond and react the same way we would, which couldn't be farther from a genuine response. So we allow them to respond in whatever way they see fit. We take this data and we move accordingly. We want customers to want to spend their currency and exchange energy with us, because they want to, not because there is this false sense of an obligation. I must admit, the climate of the era we are living in has led us to the point where we are "safer" mentally, just not expecting things. This includes business, not expecting loyalty; but definitely appreciating loyal customers. I am very grateful for all of our customers and much love to our family and friends that do support. Its love!

2.   Always be *willing & ready* to fund your dreams; dream big, dream often.

One thing I learned after I set a few goals for myself was to dream big and dream often. A lot of times there has been an imaginary ceiling that people, friends, parents, family, school systems, religions, and basic indoctrination has placed over our lives. I've met a lot of people that didn't even realize that they could literally do whatever it is they want in this life. Too many times has our lives been set for us and left us with very little choices and very little control over the way we want our lives to go; at least that's what we were led to think. This can build resentment and lead to misplaced anger because we are not doing what we want or dreamed for ourselves. Many of times our mind and emotions are directing us in a way we want to go, and everything we learned at an early age has been given to us in a way to go against that very inner voice telling us to go out and be happy. A lot of times this confusion can be led back to birth. It was at that very moment you were given a bottle instead of your mothers breast, the confusion began.

We should experience everything we can in this lifetime. The soul wants to go on the journey it was sent here for. A lot of time us listening to this inner intuition and that inner voice is what will lead us to that place of peace, love, joy, and happiness. These tips have been the key to allowing myself to dream and actually remember them. By removing restrictions from the mind, body, and soul we allow ourselves to be free. A free vessel dreams more, and experience this realm in a way it was truly designed to.

One thing I reflect on is the goals I set for myself when I was 15 years old. I wanted a nice house, my mom opened me a savings account and I remember giving her my first 50 dollars to put into my savings account; that was the first 50 that went toward my house fund, I was only 15. When I was 21, we began construction on that very house and had it was complete when I was 22. We still live in this house today. While this was a huge accomplishment, I look back and know that in those moments, if I had dreamt bigger, there wasn't a doubt in my mind that I could have had more. I feel I could have dreamed more. When I walked into consciousnesses I soon realized that the real work took place in the dream world and the daily things we experience was the actual dream, so yes, we're awake, living the dream. This is where I go to "prepare a place". I was able to go directly into a dream and literally alter my future, some things were as recent as a few hours later and some a bit further into the future. It is quite amazing to watch the things we dream of in another reality be inserted and come to fruition in our Earth realm, and we get to share it with the ones we love the most.

In the world we live in there are many ways to ensure our dreams are tangible, sometimes these things take money. Yes the same money we touched on earlier. One huge handicap I've noticed in this American experience is the use of two things, that's Cash App and GoFundMe. People have used and abused these two money magnets and replaced the grind and hustle with the need to ask and beg others to share their hard earned money and energy and contribute to theirs due to their lack of preparedness. I recall hearing this a while back, "if you fail to plan, you plan to fail". Have a plan for anything you want in this life and go after it. Don't follow your dreams, chase your dreams.

I remember wanting some things for myself so bad until I was literally in tears, and impatient many times. Often I think people simply don't have the drive or just don't want it bad enough. When someone wants something bad enough, they will go through just about anything and at any extreme to bring it to them. The way I see it, as long as it doesn't exceed your boundaries, go for it. I ask myself a couple questions, is it illegal, immoral, or unethical (based on my knowing), more than likely it isn't, and then I proceed.

I don't typically follow the rules; I own my soul, not the things around me, I experience the things around me. This allows me to maneuver this life in a way that is free of fear, guilt, and judgement. Many times those are the factors that keep us in a certain mindset and bound to the lower realms of consciousness. Everything that I want, I am willing to do what I deem necessary to get it. I am willing to do it alone, I am willing to set a schedule or work extended hours to do so. As a kid I washed cars. Learned mechanic work. My uncle taught me carpentry. That led to plumbing. I was always curious about electricity, I began to learn that trade too. There was a time where I was doing all of these jobs and saving every dime to put toward my dreams and goals. I did whatever it took. Worked long hours, took on extra jobs, lost countless hours of sleep, maybe its just the Capricorn in me, but the drive to get what I came here for tends to float to the front and that's all I'm focused on in that moment (yes this can be good and bad at times). Be willing to balance this life in this short small amount of uncertain time. Work for the things we want, balance this with the opportunity to share this experience with the ones we love, our kids, family, friends. Everything won't come at the snap of the finger but be willing and prepared to put in the work and create a plan that will allow us to achieve the things we want, even set milestones and targets that will help you in the this pursuit. I tell myself, I deserve everything I'm willing to work for. I see a divine reflection in everything I want and everything I do.

3. Always listen to your "Haters/Complainers"; they'll tell you *honest* things your friends won't.

Have you ever knew deep down inside you was making the wrong decision and asked a friend about about it and they encouraged you to go through with it? Our friends and family or even a random person will not always tell us what we need to hear, some just tell us what we want to hear. It is good to identify these things with the people we spend time with and value their opinions. I have people I know will not tell me the truth if their life depended on it. I also have the friends that I know who will tell me what I need to hear and not what I want to hear. I've come to a point where I can take the hard conversations and criticism and build on it in an effort to show up a better and more healed version of myself (yes I had trauma I had to process too).

There's a reason corporations ask you to fill out surveys. How many people actually fill out a survey without either having a really good experience, or a terrible one that just made you fill out the paperwork. A lot times the most truthful and constructive critiques will come from the customer with the 1-rating. It's good to even get that information while the emotions are high and fresh; let them get it all out. Evaluate the data you just received and determine what can change within your business that can eleveate this potential problem in the future. When necessary, do what is required to save a loyal customer.

As the owner we accept all responsibility over our business. No matter how big, no matter how small. I've had to give a customer a free meal, their money back, and another free meal when they returned because of a mistake that I made. When its over I simply thank them for the opportunity to make it right. Have you ever went somewhere, didn't have a good experience and when you told the right person, they accommodated or discounted your meal, or even gave it to you free? Are you more likely to return? What about when you had a bad experience and didn't tell anyone? Did you return? Likely you didn't, you probably said to yourself, "they aint gotta see me here again". I mention that because when business owners value their customers and their business, they will do what is needed to make it right with their customers, and the only way this can be done is through effective communication. Rather this be through a survey or by telling a manager in person exactly how you feel; I try my best to allow them the opportunity to make things right.

There has been an instance where I would have corrected an issue, but I didnt know about it until weeks later. The customer never stated they were unsatisfied with their product. The other side of this is simple, some customers be straight up tripping and delusional, yes I said it that way on purpose. Some will try to take advantage of your problem solving resolutions. I have had customers eat their entire meals and come back just to say well it was alright, but I didn't really like it, yet they ate the entire meal and want their money back. Yea, that aint gone happen. This same customer stated they didn't like something one time and we refunded their money. They tried two other times before we cut them off. They are still a recurring customer; however, they don't push the issue about getting another free meal.

We value the opinion of all customers and welcome any information that can streamline processes or make the business better. A lot of times, friends tend to agree or tell you things like, yeah you're doing a great job, just keep up the hard work. When we are in a state of evolution and evaluation, the last thing you're trying to do is stay the same. We need constant change. We are said to be creatures of habit. We enjoy being comfortable. Change and growth doesn't always happen in a cool, comfortable, or cozy location. It's hard to heal in the same environment that hurt us. It's not impossible, it may require more focus and additional protective measures, but it's not impossible.

Nothing is the same as it were a moment ago. The stars are never in the same exact spot twice. The moments we know as past, present, ,and future as exist at the same time. We must grasp this concept and bend it to our liking. I have heard many times that I can be my biggest critic, and I don't see anything wrong with that. Surround yourself with intelligent and liked minded individuals who don't mind giving you an honest view on life and your business. And never, always be the smartest person in the room. Be around people who you can learn from. Remain teachable, remain a student.

There is a saying that sticks with me and I repeat often, it goes, "The day we please everyone, will be the day we lose ourselves". Sometimes we just gotta say forget those people and keep it stepping. Everything aint for everybody, and my business or my food may not be for you. And that's alright. Me and my personality aint for everybody, and that's alright too, but that's also not my problem. I have found many things within and I am at rest in my body. I suggested they do the same too.

4. Always separate the ***message*** from the ***messenger***; know exactly what it is you're listening to, there's always something to learn.

Too many times we have been given the concept that the only messenger that can have deliver a decent message or anything of substance is if it came from a "healed" wholesome perfect person with this perfect life who never made a mistake ever in life. Regardless of what religion and indoctrination has taught us, they gave us these people and images for a specific purpose. Eventually they know we will begin to seek these images and replicate the things they may have done and look up to them for different reasons and purposes. Having an overstanding that everything is always working for our greater good, we have to come to a point where we can decipher and extract a divine message and substance from our worst enemy. There is always something to learn, even if it is simply what not to do in a similar situation.

In the world of business the messenger can come in many forms. The quietest customer can deliver a gut punching message with their facial expressions. That same customer being a recurring customer says a lot as it is. it's been noted that the best marketing is word of mouth. When you have people talking about your product, that goes further than any tv commercial. Another example that has been held close to me is this story that I was told about "practicing what you preach". If a preacher told you to quit drinking but you witness them drinking from time to time, how would you feel. If you seen a drunkard on side of the road stumbling and barely coherent and that person told you about drinking and you should quit, what story hits closer to home and more likely to sway you to more responsible behavior. The drunkard telling you not to drink but also being a living and walking testament of what you can become if you can't get it together. Both individuals delivering a very powerful and serious message; however, the impact was different because of the messenger. This is just another way that we must find the value and the message that's being presented at the time. Who would be more qualified for assisting in breaking an addiction, someone who has never been addicted or an addict who has recovered and doing well? The same for mending a broken heart, someone who has healed from a similar situation or someone who has never experienced this.

This is a fine line that western medicine has in a way projected that the only help or value that is viable must come from a teacher from one of their universities or from a doctor. This is a huge mind bog for many and they will only receive a message from that type of messenger. We are even at the point now where people will only receive information if it is brought with a reference or resource. A lot of information I pull from the elements or nature. When we are attentive to our surroundings and in full awareness the data and information is there. Even if this is something we may want to share with our family or community, we may have to be ready to defend or support the information and include how we received it. We can get into that later.

5. Allow your customers to create items or menu options; this is just as much their business as it is yours. ***Reciprocity*** goes a long way.

One thing that I have done since Ive been in business is allow my loyal customers to always have an opinion on the menu. We have such a diverse menu, so many different options, vegan, soul food, you name it. I work in the food industry so the menu is the key for many. I never built my business with the intention of having friends and family as my sole supporters. I do think that's a big misconception for anyone getting into a business with the expectation of their friends or families being key customers or supporters. While I have been very fortunate to provide a service that my friends and family enjoy and support, I do know that's a rare occasion.

I have witnessed and read many stories of failed or failing businesses and one of the responses I noted is that one of the top reasons the person would mention is the lack of support from friends and families. Depending on culture and ethnicity this can look very different. When it comes to the world of business and entrepreneurship in America there are some very hard and disturbing truths that are present and relevant that one must know and be willing to accept. I always open my mind to the thought and relationship that business and customers share, this is just as much theirs as it is mine. I owe it to them to show up consistently with a great tasting product as much as I show up with the expectation that someone will make a purchase. There are many times that I bless the meals and food as I prepare it with the knowing that this food will spark a great feeling and loving emotion for the person receiving. With that intention, and me putting that out in the ethers, it never fails that at least one customer will come back and say that the meal that they had previously reminded them of something that a family member that they dearly missed or had transitioned had once prepared.

We live for experiences and memories, every memory is data, now how it registers in the mind and throughout the body is personal. It's for us to extract the best from every moment and build on the life we are currently experiencing. Allowing customers to have a say so on the daily operations gives them a sense of ownership and welcoming. These are the foundations that create a relationship that will be long lasting. This is reciprocity, we give them something, they give us something; balance. This is a principle that I took to heart. I began to give things to the world and the world returned the favor immediately. I learned the same thing with grace, I began to give myself grace and my surroundings were graceful with me. I gave love to my craft, and my customers returned the same energy. These aren't just business principles and practices, but I transferred these things into my everyday life and personal relationships and it has been working amazing for me. Reciprocity goes a long way. We have a deep divine connection to everything that surrounds us. Everything is push and pull, everything is love. Everything is everything. I am all things and all things are within me, therefore I deserve to have all things and all things deserve me. Balance, love. Reciprocity.

6. The ***heart*** and the ***mind*** are one, too much of either can mislead you into an emotional & irrational decision⚖. Never make a business decision personal.

There are many ancient and sacred teachings that break down the many trifectas that surround mankind, human beings, or whatever it is you refer to this existence as. One of the most interesting yet revealing is the mind, body, and soul. From my understanding of these three is that they complete the essence of who we are. The mind is housed throughout or in multiple places within the body. The soul is housed within the body; the soul wants to be at rest in the body. This is one of our missions while we have the conscious awareness, creating the environment where the soul can be at rest within the body, this where we find peace even in the midst of a storm. This can be quite difficult if we rely on things outside of ourselves to complete and identify cycles within our lives; this is why some people's life, mental, and emotional state can be chaotic.

The major chakras of the body can assist in understanding more aspects of our mind, body, and soul, and the alignment that is required to ensure we can prosper in a peaceful resting state. Too much into the mind and we can overthink and overanalyze any situation. Too much into the body, or relying on the heart can lead us into giving away too much or allowing others to take advantage of us. So simply put, to allow the soul to rest at home, we must balance the many versions and variables of self, aligning the body, processing information, collecting data, preserving the life force energy and being in total control or total awareness.

When we are in total control we tend to make better decisions. These decisions on behalf of our business will be solid, fluent, and in the best interest of the company; not irrational or emotional. When it comes to this, we must remind ourself to take these decisions personal, yes these two intersect and ride a fine line. I constantly remind myself not to take certain things personal. It's been stated that cooler heads prevail, we tend to hear that in the sports world. So I breath, take a few moments to myself before I make big decisions. If additional time is needed, I simply ask and if they cannot accommodate I make the best decision, in the best time, based on the best information I had in the best moment, and we live with the outcome. When playing chess, there are many variables we must consider and forward thinking at least five moves; this is how I consider new options for the business. Visionaries and progressive leaders that separate personal from business are what's needed to advance a company in the todays world.

Ask yourself, is my soul at rest in my body. Is my body in a stable place where it can be at rest? Now ask that same question regarding the business; what the mind does, the body follows. The energy flows, where the attention goes.

7.   Always, take care of those, who take care of you. We're here to *experience* each other.

Taking care of those who take care of you didn't seem like a hard feel at first glimpse, but I felt the need to tap into this one because I watch a lot of people continue to support businesses that do not, have not, ever, ever taken care of them. How many times has that business that you support oh so faithfully donated back or sewed back into the community that its erected (and some times directed) in? When was the last time you witnessed one of your daily stops set up in the community giving anything back; charities, churches, school supplies, clothes? In todays time its rare to see anyone outside just simply giving back to their community because it felt like the right thing to do. A lot of the issues we have in our communities and families are due to psychological blockages where we have yet to see the reflection of ourselves in our neighbors. This in my opinion makes it easier for us to mistreat each other.

Taking care of those who took care of me hit when someone stopped me one day and said they were glad I didn't become a product of my environment. It took me a second to really think about this because the only reason I am the way I am today and has made it to this point is because of my environment. So therefore, I am a product of my environment; I just make it look different based off my choices. My business Droptop BBQ was created of the same idea of taking care of those who took care of me. One day I pulled my smoker to the road and gave away free BBQ to anyone who would stop. At the time I wasn't reminded of the vision of owning a business one day and what it looked liked. But I just wanted to give back to my neighborhood and show them what type of products we were producing. Soon after when I decided to turn the bbq into a business, a lot the people who I gave free BBQ to were some of my daily customers. I gained a lot of clientele, friends, and family's trust with the meals from a first encounter that was a giveaway; they still shop to this day.

Theres a beautiful dance we tend to do with our customers, we provide something, they provide something. I began to look at everything as a spiritual experience and every chance I encounter another vessel, our spirits get the opportunity to converse and dance, then we maneuver accordingly. Regardless of the type of mood someone may be in, I always think of our encounter as a divine occasion. Just knowing that we are here to experience each other I continue to find value in everything and everyone I come into contact with. I think of the person as a new experience but a divine reflection of me. My perception of the good, the bad, the ugly, the fast, the slow, the mediocre. If I don't get it together I can become that person; if I continue the work I can become that person too.

8. Competition can be healthy; it'll keep you in a constant state of *evaluation & evolution*. $\boxed{\circlearrowleft}$

Competition is the thing that can keep businesses in the state of evolution. When there is a need to reevaluate the day to day processes or just the needs of the customers, this is space for growth. Not only does the business go through evolution, but the customers do as well. The business should always suit the needs and wants of its customers. This is why we must pay close attention to the things that are happening around us (awareness). Typically the first to enter the market in a supply and demand versus scarcity or proximity will be the biggest winner. But as soon as a need arises or a solution is present we must know that there are others watching and will want a piece of the pie. This does not mean that one single person can "own" an industry. There will be multiple businesses erupt and other owners will do what they feel is necessary to put their own spin on it (some will take your business structure and try to duplicate it identically so protecting your business is a must too). These are the small details that will make each business unique.

As crazy as it sounds I have had other people come to me and state "I see what you doing out here and see the money you're making, just know after while, you're going to have to slide over because I'm coming or a piece of that". Yes someone told me this. Truly, what can I do? Other than continue to provide the best product I possibly can, I can look to the customers and ask how are we meeting their needs. See if there are other things they would like to see, any changes or special requests. We as humans have shown to be creatures of habit and we enjoy comfort. The evolution process, a lot of times, is uncomfortable. Growth and change does not always feel or look good, nor will it look the same for every person or each business.

Understanding numerology has shown that "death" is simply another transition to rebirth. As we remember this, we understand that we transition from phase to phase and from cycle to cycle many times in the lifespan of different things in life. We must continuously evaluate, take notes, collect data, and make the changes we see fit, not being afraid to close the door, close the book, or close the chapter that has ended.

The next question, when do we need to make the changes, there's a simple answer for that too. You make the changes or accept the risk, when the benefits outweigh the cost. We should continuously think about those two factors or variables... benefits and costs. The art of being uncomfortable is something that this business taught me. I have seen many businesses start and end, open and close, new businesses, major franchises, old business. They all had to accept the fact that it was more beneficial for them to close or shift their business. Rather that was due to the location or maybe the upper management or leadership changed, or maybe the needs of the community changed and their services were no longer needed. To have longevity in any business it is important to embed yourself into the culture of the customers or the community. As you look around at businesses today, you see exactly that, they have created a need for you as the customer to need them. You can look around in your community and identify many issues or problems you may have. I tell people, we don't have problems, we have job opportunities. We turn these problems into opportunities when we create the solution and begin to charge for our solutions.

Another important thing to remember is to protect the investment or the solution so that it may be yours (legally), because others will notice and come running for whatever the light that you have shining is illuminating. There is a cycle that I use when looking to my business; that is self, family, community, culture. The culture should solve the problems that are in the community in some way. So your businesses should live in the culture of the people who are in that community. Do you have to look outside of your community to solve a problem that resides within your community? If you do that is a problem in itself, and that means that you are embedded in another community's culture where they are relying on your spending to support their community or simply to keep you subservient. This is a big factor that plagues specific ethnic groups who don't have access to certain profitable resources. This is also an indication that there is a physiological evaluation that may need to be done on the people of that community, both communities at that. Without going too deep into the history of how certain groups arrived to that point, it is more important to know that other groups have been studying other groups of people for this very reason and they do not mind studying them for generations. Then they wait for the ideal time to do what they need, to embed themselves in the perfect places that will last and benefit them for generations, off the backs of the people in that area. To understand history is to understand the psychology and the mind of the people who wrote it; always look to both sides for a full evaluation. In easier terms, use the competition as a means to fuel your evolution. Also understand, you don't own the industry.

We hear a lot about capitalism, and the negative effects of it. I would encourage people to see exactly what true capitalism is and compare that to what it is you are currently experiencing. Capitalism insists that the trade industry is controlled by private owners for a profit. So I ask you again, is it truly capitalism that we are experiencing? Likely, its is not. We are dealing with an insidious monopoly that is controlled by government, religion, and a few individuals with lots of money and power that has bought out the smaller or private sector and created another system. The quick fix is rarely the correct answer for issues that live in our worlds. This same need for quick fixes and poverty is the same study that has been done on our people and this allows for the government and that small group of rich and powerful people to swoop in with a resolution, some money, and save the day. Ultimately allowing us to play to our very own demise, where we for generations will be dependent on them and their service they provide. Us never owning anything privately, but always looking outside of our community and culture for answers and resources for personal problems, is a problem. Create. Evaluate. Evolve.

9.   Last but not least. Never forget. *Always give thanks*! Give thanks for everything that brought you to this point; the good, bad, ugly, pretty, confusion, discipline, commitment, love, Integrity! Remember, the things that are happening *to you*, are happening *for you*; the things that are happening *for you* are happening *through you*. ♺ Live in love. Start every day fresh, *renewed of the mind!*

When I say never forget, I mean never forget the moments and the people who helped propel you to this place, to this very moment that you're reading this document. With so much that goes on in our day to day lives it is easy to forget how fragile life is, and if one single thing was different, every moment we experience could be different. Have you ever just sat back and realized how perfect of a creation we are in? Even when things don't quite seem to always be in our best interest, its always in our best interest, sometimes we don't see it while we sit in the minutia of whatever it is we are dealing with in the moment. I reflect a lot on nature and watch the sun, moon, and stars do their beautiful and quite entertaining dance daily and nightly, putting on a perfect display of balance. We watch the seasons and cycles open and close, come and go. We see the moon phases light up the night sky and even experience eclipses.

With the worries of the world it is easy to lose sight and track of the beautiful surroundings we dwell in everyday. Can you imagine what this could look like if one thing was different. If the water levels shifted, if the cosmos or sun decided to take a break? But they have been ever present exulting a vibrant energy and giving to us every thing we need to sustain life. We should be appreciative and give thanks for everything that comes our way. I mention the things we perceive to be negative, because once we get to the bottom of whatever lesson it was we were learning we found out that that very moment was very needed for us to arrive to this moment. It's important for us to know that we will not always have all the answers all the time and some things just take time. Some things hit us in the very moment we sit in the awareness, other things can take years. Some things can require us to team up with other energies to extract the information. These are all things that build on the build.

We were given a construct of time and how it was said to operate, but after doing research and taking full control of my life I found out that time as we know it surrounds me and everything I have going on. I then found out I can time travel and even speed up moments and slow then down to examine exactly what it is I want. I too found out that this concept only works for me, in my world. Have you ever looked up and thought time has flown by, but asked the person next to you and their response was the complete opposite. Time is linear, but time is also circular. Time seems to move in cycles and if we can look into this from a large enough perspective we can really see the cycles and how things move. Using simple math like pi, multiplication, division, addition, and subtraction, we can notice that time is actually cylindrical and everything is one huge moment. Day and night, hours, minutes, seconds, are all tools to assist us with aligning ourselves with other energies or people so we can better experience this thing we call life, ultimately experiencing ourself. When we view it in this way we realize that opportunities and experiences are as vast as our minds can comprehend. When we are open to the facts that we control this reality and not the government, not our spouse, not any religious organization, not our kids, not any old decision, we realize that at any moment we can will ourselves to joy. We can simply decide to live in the joys of this world.

At higher levels of consciousness it is understood that when we control this reality that nothing ever happens to you, things always seem to happen for you. But the things that happen for you are happening through you. That's one of my favorite mantras, I know this to be very true in my life. The things that are happening to me are happening for me, and the things that are happening for me are happening through me. With this being known it is clear to see that I create my reality, every aspect of it. This can be hard for some to grasp because they haven't come to the place where they are willing and ready to live with the results. There is no good or bad, there are consequences and results to our actions; the real question is can you live with it. Can you live with he results of the moves you make daily? Rather it's spades, chess, or checkers, there is always someone else's turn and always an equal or opposite reaction that can either propel or set you back, but there is always balance present. The real thing is what are we going to do with it.

Have you ever witnessed someone do pretty much the same identical thing you did, but the result was totally different for them? Some things that we receive are just for us, and no one could every duplicate the process and get the same result. Some things were meant just for us and not for us to share with the world. So enjoy your abundance, enjoy your life, it is just for you. The things we see that's perceived to be negative are results of our actions as well (most the time), we live in a world and a country that if we don't know the rules and loop holes to the game, we lose. The first person to lose the game is the person who don't know they're playing. So study this game called life and remain open to perspectives and new information. A person who knows a lot realizes he knows nothing at all, there's so much to pull and learn from. Ask questions, learn something new daily.

At any moment we can be renewed of the mind. I try to make this my rising regime. I start my day fresh with thanks for the breath and rhythm of the heart. Realizing how important the breath is is a very calming and grounding notion. Do you realize if you miss one breath, this reality as we know it is over. Do you realize that if we miss just one heartbeat, that this reality as we know it is over. If any of the systems of the body or nature decides not to work that this reality as we know it is over, or we will have a totally different outlook on it because it will be a new version of something that we've never experienced. Find the balance in the things we know, find the awareness to be aware of the unaware. Lead with love, love is the magic potion and gratitude is the gift that just keeps on giving.

Show your customers that you appreciate them. Maybe it's simply writing a letter on their box, thanks, enjoy. Leaving a mint in their bag. A small surprise will always go a long way in business. Align the energy centers and allow the mind to guide the body so the soul may be at rest... that sounds a lot like peace. This was written with love and intention. May your business thrive and your mind be at ease. I know we will find peace. Love. The Droptop way.

List 10 things you are grateful for in life, in your business

_____

_____

_____

_____

_____

_____

_____

_____

_____

_____

_____

_____

_____

_____

_____

_____

_____

_____

_____

_____

_____

_____

_____

_____

List the top five activities that bring you peace and who and how you'd rather do them with.

_____

_____

_____

_____

_____

_____

_____

_____

_____

_____

_____

_____

_____

_____

_____

_____

_____

_____

_____

_____

_____

_____

_____

_____

_____

_____

_____

_____

_____

_____

Be specific with what needs to be done to elevate your business. What can you do right now in this moment for elevation.

_____

_____

_____

_____

_____

_____

_____

_____

_____

_____

_____

_____

_____

_____

_____

_____

_____

_____

_____

_____

_____

_____

_____

_____

_____

_____

_____

Those things that you listed above, how can this be measured? Tangible, intangible, list ways you can measure the specifics.

_____

_____

_____

_____

_____

_____

_____

_____

_____

_____

_____

_____

_____

_____

_____

_____

_____

_____

_____

_____

_____

_____

_____

_____

_____

Now that you can measure the specifics, what is an attainable pace for you to progress? It's not likely you can run an engine at max speed at all times. Set goals, ensure they are attainable and sustainable. You can set multiple milestones in route to your bigger goal.

_____

_____

_____

_____

_____

_____

_____

_____

_____

_____

_____

_____

_____

_____

_____

_____

_____

_____

_____

_____

_____

_____

_____

Results are required in business; list the intended results for implementing the items previously discussed.

_____

_____

_____

_____

_____

_____

_____

_____

_____

_____

_____

_____

_____

_____

_____

_____

_____

_____

_____

_____

_____

_____

_____

_____

_____

_____

_____

_____

_____

_____

Through this journey of peace and business, it is my thoughts that you will find some peace after you complete some of the items that are on your todo list or ofter you begin to see some of the fruits of your labor. How much time do you give yourself to complete the actionable items listed above? If the targets are not accomplished, how much additional time do you give yourself to finish?

_____
_____
_____
_____
_____
_____
_____
_____
_____
_____
_____
_____
_____
_____
_____
_____
_____
_____
_____
_____
_____
_____
_____